PRAYING HANDS

THE PRAYER OF JABEZ

that Your hand w
and that You would
that I may not
So God grante
reque
I CHRONIC

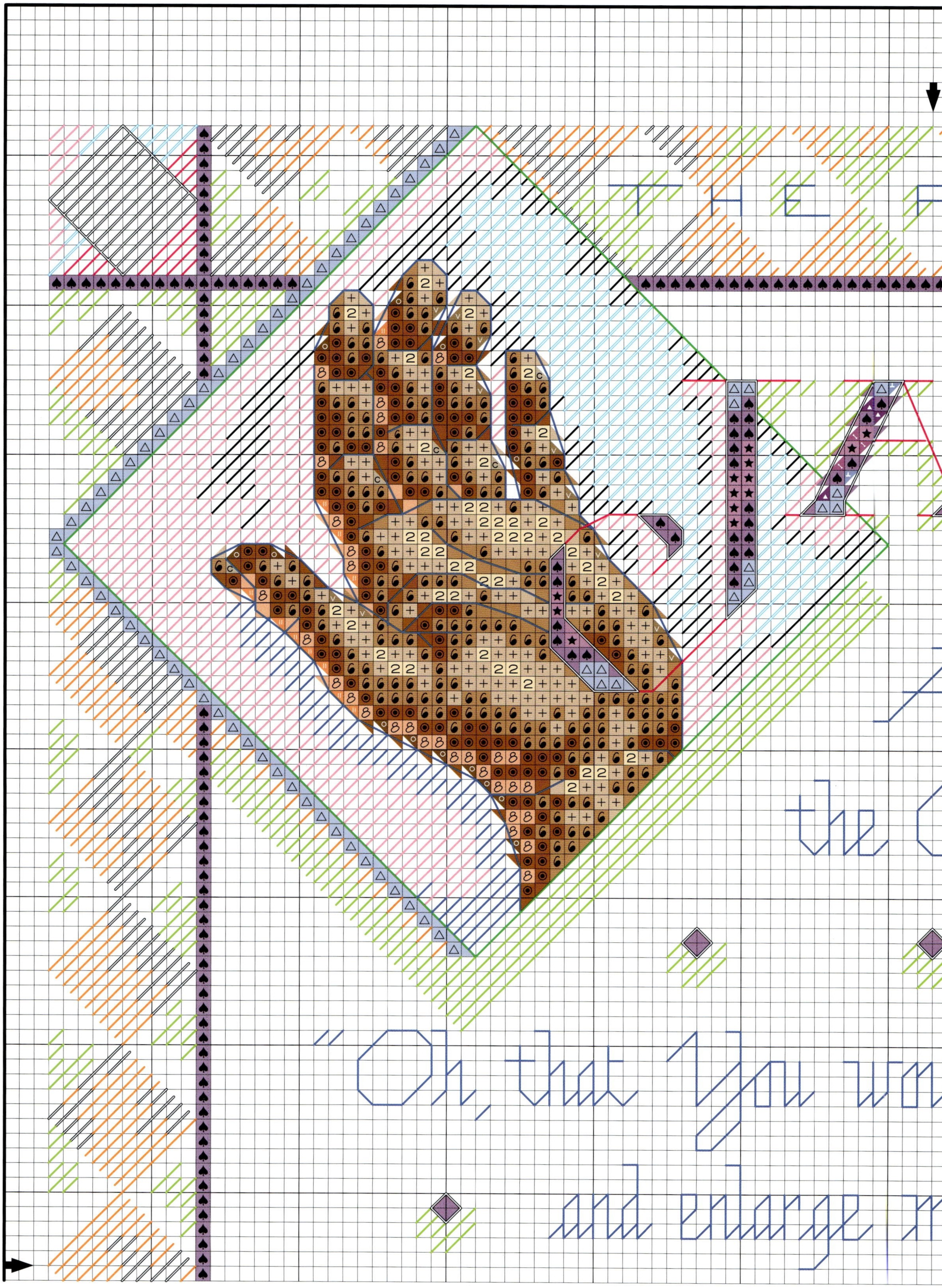
THE P
the C
"Oh, that You wou
and enlarge m

THE PRAYER OF JABEZ

Hidden amidst scores of genealogies, a brief but extraordinary passage of scripture has become widely studied as the key to living a more blessed life. Illustrated here with a majestic mountain scene and distinctive border, this inspirational project will serve as a daily reminder of the principles found in this poignant prayer.

THE PRAYER OF JABEZ (120w x 154h)

X	DMC	1/4X	3/4X	B'ST	ANC.	COLOR
	155			◪ †		lavender
✳	[156			◪ □		lt blue
	*793				176	blue
△	158	◪	◪	◪ †		vy dk blue
♠	327	◪	◪	◪ ★	100	dk purple
	327			◪ ○	100	dk purple
n	341			◪ †	117	lt blue
◉	407	◪	◪		914	dk flesh
⁘	422				943	gold
♦♦	519			◪ +	1038	turquoise
	792			◪ ◇	941	dk blue
¢	827			◪ □	160	lt turquoise
6	950	◪	◪		4146	flesh
+	951	◪	◪		1010	lt flesh
□	3042			◪ ♡	870	vy lt purple
♥	3362			◪ +	263	dk green
⊖	3363			◪ ◇	262	green
$	3364				260	lt green
	3746			◪ □	1030	violet
2	3823			◪ +	386	lt gold
♦	3828			◪	373	dk gold
	3828			◪ Δ	373	dk gold
★	3835	◪	◪	◪ ★	98	purple
↑	3836				90	lt purple
	3860			◪ ◇	379	taupe
8	[3860	◪	◪		379	taupe
	*3861				378	lt taupe
✓	3863			◪ ○	379	brown
	202HL#4			◪ ○		Kreinik metallic very fine braid
	202HL#12			◪ ♡		Kreinik metallic tapestry braid
•	792					dk blue Fr. Knot

Δ Use **1** strand of floss.

* Use **2** strands of first floss color listed and **1** of the second.

† DMC 155 behind hand. DMC 158 for corners. DMC 341 in border.

★ DMC 327 for wording. DMC 3835 for corners.

○ DMC 327 for wording and small diamonds (**1** strand). Kreinik 202HL #4 Braid for corners (**1** strand). DMC 3863 in border.

\+ DMC 519 behind hand. DMC 3823 for sky. DMC 3362 for border.

◇ DMC 792 for wording and behind hand. DMC 3860 for hand (**1** strand). DMC 3363 for border.

□ DMC 827 behind hand. DMC 3746 for corners. DMC 156/793 blend for border (Use **1** strand of each floss color listed).

♡ Kreinik 202HL #12 Braid (**1** strand) couched with **1** strand of 202HL #4 Braid for border around large diamond. DMC 3042 for all other in border.

The Prayer of Jabez was stitched on a 15" x 17" piece of 28 count Tea-dyed Linen (design size 8⅝" x 11") over two fabric threads. Three strands of floss were used for Cross Stitch and 2 strands for French Knots and Backstitch except where noted in color key. It was custom framed.

The Prayer of Jabez (120w x 154h)

14 count	8⅝"	x	11"
16 count	7½"	x	9⅝"
18 count	6¾"	x	8⅝"

STITCHES

Beginning and Ending Stitches — When beginning or ending a length of floss, always secure the floss end under stitches; never tie knots. At the beginning of a row of cross stitches, leave a tail of floss on the back of fabric and stitch over it with the first few cross stitches. This will secure the end. When ending a length of floss, run the floss under several stitches on the back of fabric to secure (Diagram A).

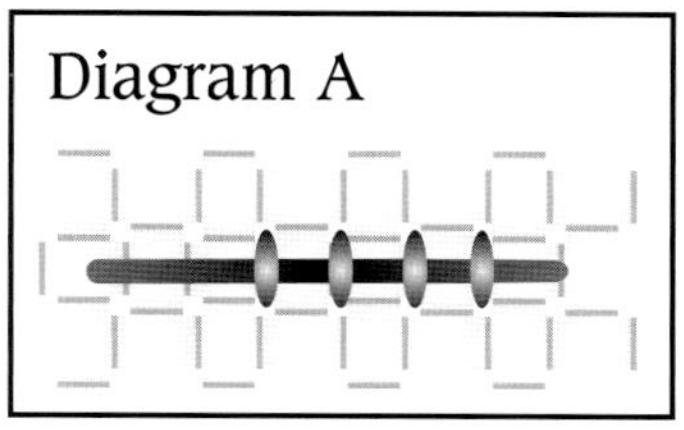
Diagram A

Cross Stitch — When working stitches in a horizontal row, follow numbers in Diagram B to work stitches from left to right and then back again. When working stitches vertically, follow numbers in Diagram C to complete each stitch before you move down to work the next stitch. When working stitches over two fabric threads on linen or similar fabrics, follow numbers in Diagram D.

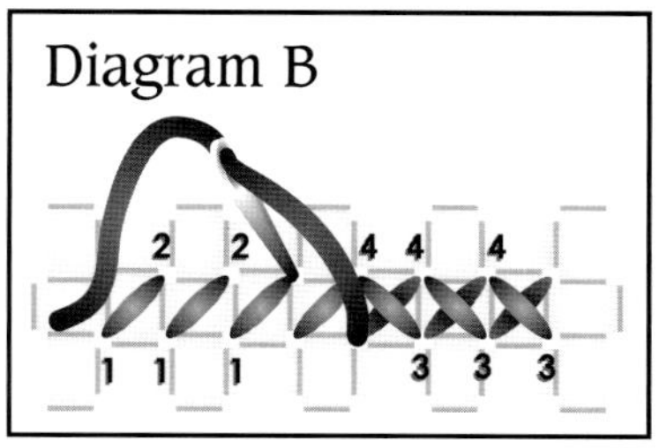
Diagram B

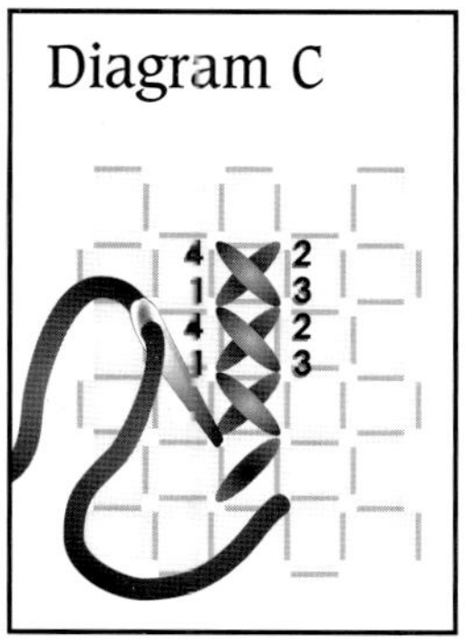
Diagram C

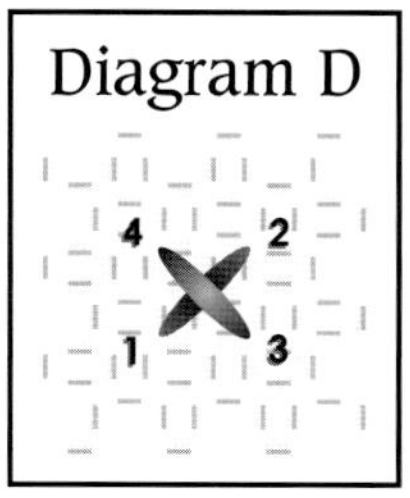
Diagram D

One-Quarter Stitch — Work one-quarter of a Cross Stitch, splitting the fabric threads when working on Aida (Diagram E) or only crossing one thread when working over two threads on linen or similar fabrics (Diagram F).

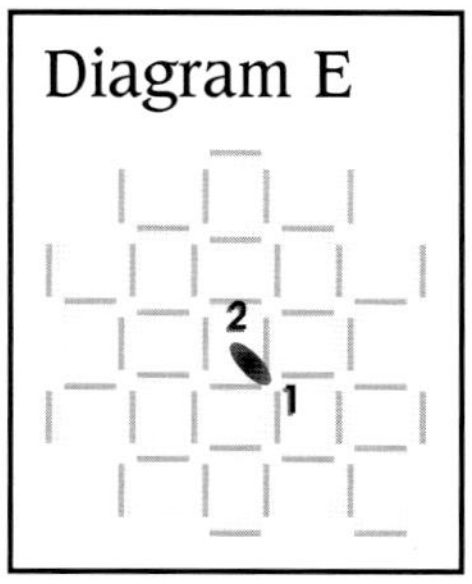
Diagram E

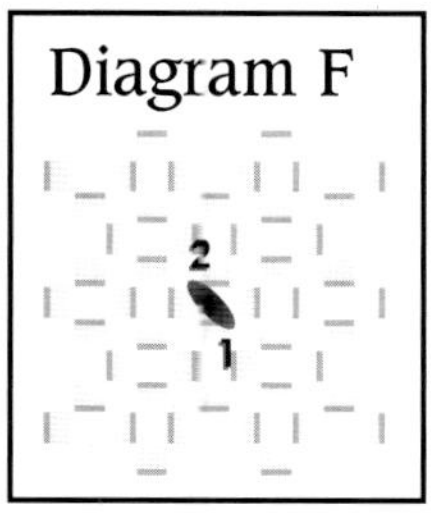
Diagram F

Three-Quarter Stitch — Work three-quarters of a Cross Stitch by following numbers in Diagram G when working on Aida. Follow numbers in Diagram H when working over two threads on linen or similar fabrics.

Diagram G

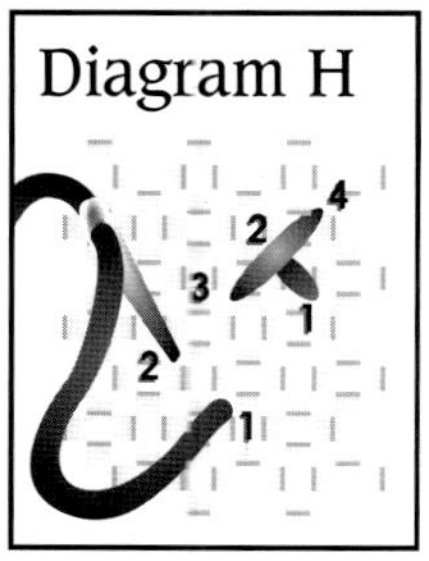
Diagram H

Backstitch — Work backstitching after all cross stitching is completed. Follow numbers in Diagram I when working Backstitch on Aida. Follow numbers in Diagram J when working over two threads on linen or similar fabrics.

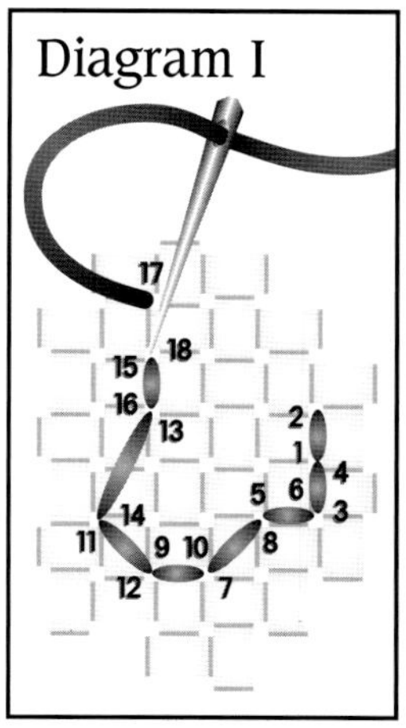
Diagram I

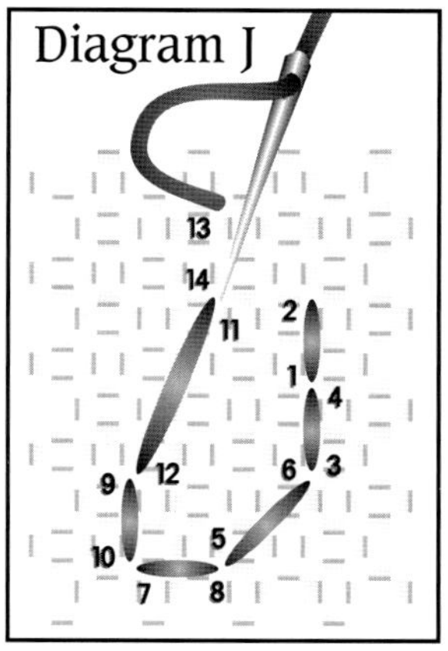
Diagram J

Couching — Following numbers in Diagram K, use 1 strand of tapestry braid for long stitch and 1 strand of very fine braid for tie-down stitches.

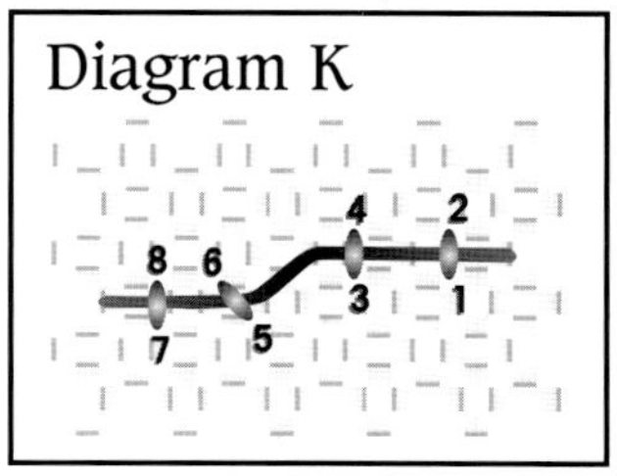
Diagram K

French Knot — Follow numbers in Diagram L to bring needle up at 1. Wind floss once around needle and take needle down at 2, holding loose end of floss tight until knot is formed.

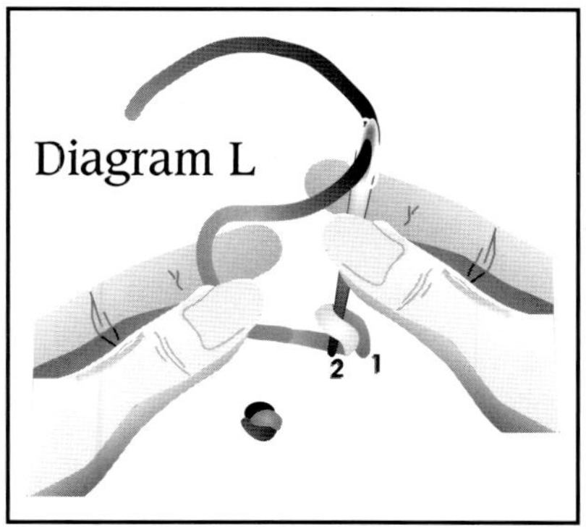
Diagram L

Design by Sandy Orton.

Fabric provided courtesy of Charles Craft Inc.
Embroidery floss provided courtesy of The DMC Corporation.

RAYER OF
BEZ
And Jabez called on
God of Israel saying,
ld bless me indeed,
y territory,

uld be with me,
d keep me from evil,
t cause pain!"
d him what he
sted
LES 4:10

PRAYING HANDS COLLECTION

BEST SELLERS

Leaflet 24012

Leaflet 24018

Leaflet 24016

Leaflet 24017

Leaflet 24006

Leaflet 24003

Leaflet 24010

Leaflet 24009

Leaflet 24019

ISBN 1-57486-975-2
PRAYER OF JABEZ
90000
9 781574 869750